Hanukkah

Lori Dittmer

seedlings

CREATIVE EDUCATION • CREATIVE PAPERBACKS

Published by Creative Education and Creative Paperbacks
P.O. Box 227, Mankato, Minnesota 56002
Creative Education and Creative Paperbacks are imprints of
The Creative Company
www.thecreativecompany.us

Design by Ellen Huber; production by Colin O'Dea
Art direction by Rita Marshall
Printed in the United States of America

Photographs by Alamy (Peter Horree), Getty Images
(John Block/Photolibrary, Cavan Images, fhm/Moment,
motimeiri/iStock), iStockphoto (christopherconrad, Instants,
jcphoto, Kameleon007, LPETTET, lucky-photographer,
motimeiri, RBOZUK, stray_cat, supercat67, John Theodor,
tovfla, traveler1116, tunart, YekoPhotoStudio), Shutterstock
(Africa Studio)

Library of Congress Cataloging-in-Publication Data
Names: Dittmer, Lori, author.
Title: Hanukkah / Lori Dittmer.
Series: Seedlings.
Includes index.
Summary: A kindergarten-level introduction to Hanukkah,
covering the holiday's history, popular traditions, and such
defining symbols as the menorah and the dreidel.
Identifiers: LCCN: 2019053307 / ISBN 978-1-64026-330-7
(hardcover) / ISBN 978-1-62832-862-2 (pbk) / ISBN 978-1-
64000-460-3 (eBook)
Subjects: LCSH: Hanukkah—Juvenile literature.
Classification: LCC BM695.H3 D57 2020 / DDC 296.4/35—dc23

CCSS: RI.K.1, 2, 3, 4, 5, 6, 7; RI.1.1,
2, 3, 4, 5, 6, 7; RF.K.1, 3; RF.1.1

TABLE OF CONTENTS

Hello, Hanukkah! **4**

When Is Hanukkah? **6**

Holiday Symbols **8**

Taking Back the Temple **10**

Long-lasting Candles **12**

Holiday Food **14**

How Do People Celebrate? **16**

Goodbye, Hanukkah! **18**

Picture Hanukkah **20**

Words to Know **22**

Read More **23**

Websites **23**

Index **24**

Hello,
Hanukkah!

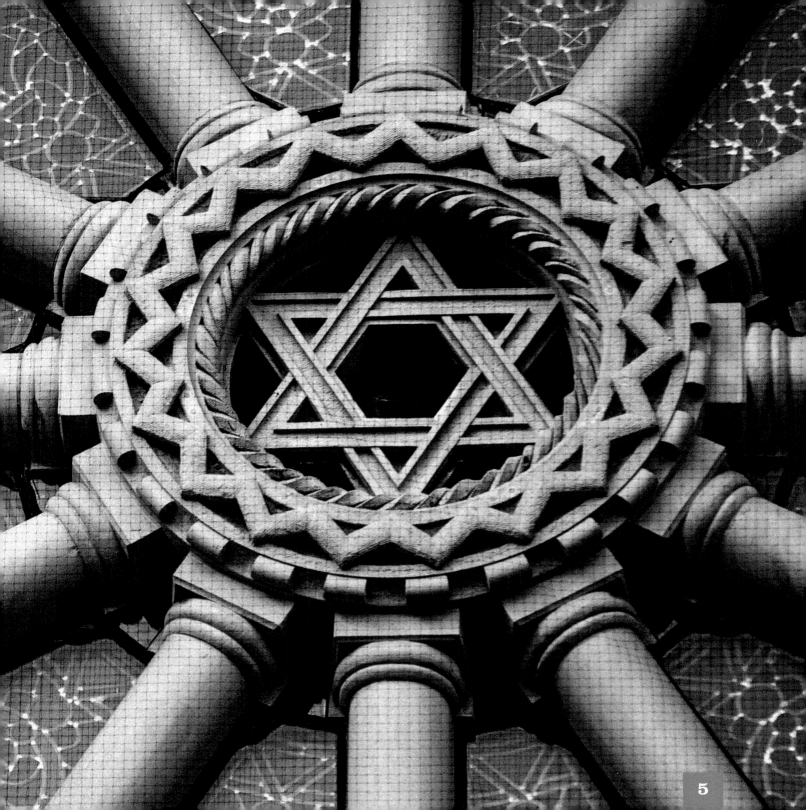

Hanukkah is a Jewish holiday. It usually begins in December.

Star of David

It lasts for eight nights and days. It is also called the Festival of Lights.

A menorah holds nine candles.

A dreidel is a spinning top. Each side has a letter on it.

Long ago, the Jewish people fought a king.

They took back their city.

The people lit candles in their temple.

The candles should have lasted only one day. But they burned for eight days!

Many Hanukkah
foods are fried in oil.

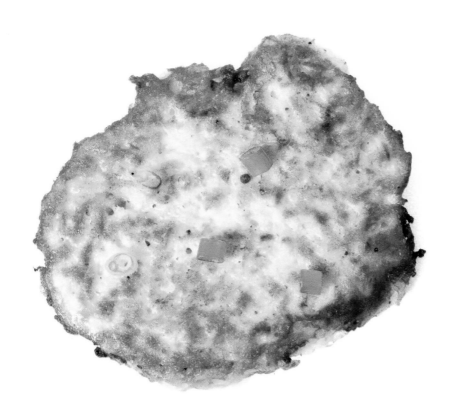

People enjoy jelly doughnuts and potato pancakes.

Families play a dreidel game.

They light candles.
Loved ones give each
other presents.

Goodbye,

Hanukkah!

menorah

dreidel

chocolate coins

latkes

Jewish: relating to Jews, people whose religion is Judaism

menorah: a candleholder used during Hanukkah

temple: a building used for worship

Read More

Amstutz, Lisa J. *Hanukkah*.
North Mankato, Minn.: Capstone, 2017.

Grack, Rachel. *Hanukkah*.
Minneapolis: Bellwether Media, 2017.

Websites

National Geographic Kids: Winter Celebrations
https://kids.nationalgeographic.com/explore/winter
-celebrations/
Read more about Hanukkah and other winter celebrations.

YouTube: The Story of Hanukkah
https://www.youtube.com/watch?v=7tws_uMAEOs
Watch a video about the history of Hanukkah.

Index

candles **8, 12, 13, 17**

Festival of Lights **7**

foods **14, 15**

history **10–11, 12–13**

symbols **8, 9, 16, 17**

temples **12**

timing **6–7**

traditions **16, 17**